POEMS TO BE WRITTEN

Sonia Quintero

Published by

SONESQUIN

London, UK
2019

POEMS TO BE WRITTEN

Sonia Quintero

This book is an invitation to interact and connect my writing and your creativity.

I would like to share my journey and invite you to create your own, reclaiming the empty space to write your story.

It is a collaborative poetry book and here it is how it works:

My poems only have a number and you are invited to name them.

Use the empty page next to each poem to write, draw, create a collage or anything the poem inspires you.

Then share it, if you wish, with @sonesquin on Instagram.

Wish you a creative life!

1.

I see poets

I saw poets where others saw failures
I saw pens and paper where others saw chaos
I saw through the eyes of Cupid himself
I saw you and then I loved you

Because

I see the wings of humming birds whispering
sonnets that only you could hear
I see privileged creators where others see losers
I see eternal souls where others see shadows
and bodies
I see hands, magic hands transforming paper and
ink into art
I see your hands
I see them like birds in the desert
I see them circling baron lands to discover what
others cannot imagine.
I see you and I still love you.

I see poets...

2.

Your hands

      Together

         Pray

Your hands

      Individually

         Write

Your hands

      My hands

         Together

      Make love

         Create the world

3.

Words are broken wings

of an extinct bird,

the one that was killed for the civilized being.

They are dead bodies,

ghosts looking for an empty place to try to be

born again.

Words are broken wings,

they are limited, narrow,

sometimes

they are a contraction

an inhalation, exhalation

an expansion, explosion.

Words are broken wings,

they are a box that I need to use

to express what I cannot apprehend.

Words are chains.

4.

Copy, repeat

Copy, cut, repeat

Copy, cut, run, repeat

Copy, repeat

You and I will never be the same.

5.

Don't stop the magician.

Don't call them jugglers,

come and try to keep the balance when life falls apart, come and smile so loud that the world wakes up.

Don't call me a poet.

Don't stop the chaos,

come and share your silliness with the genius that creates the sorrows, come and destroy the ephemeral things, come (don't) love the wild.

Don't live life in sanity.

Come and believe that magic happens when two who believe in it, meet in the unknown world, the circus that never stop.

6.

You have made a mistake
I said poets, not puppets
I said rebellious, not followers

Don't misread the messenger
Don't confuse my weakness with stupidity
I have pen and paper
Through them, I found my voice

You have made a mistake
I said help us, not buy us
I said creators, no losers

Don't pretend you don't listen
Cause I can talk or shout
I can write or kill
Don't pretend you misunderstood and
always remember:
We are poets, no puppets.

7.

Poetry hurts you,

words tie your hands

and the ink runs through your mouth.

Painful paper, empty...

Waiting for a hug.

Anonymous creators,

they are hidden behind stories

which hide pain through syllables and verse.

Poetry hurts you,

do forgive the hands that touch your soul.

8.

Created my final master piece;

write nothing, paint emptiness.

Destroy it, after creating it.

They will be the last

after them, nothing can come

because everything has been done.

Loving this empty space

where life meet death and

the eternal marriage is done.

The last piece of art:

Oneness *with the* nothingness

9.

Looking for who I was

I found out who I wasn't

Looking for your soul

I lost mine

10.

I can't make you happy
regardless how hard I try.

There is always dust in your eyes
always memories of an old grief,
moments that I never lived, I cannot heal it.

Your satisfaction is unreachable,
and my hands are small and soft.
They can only touch your face your cheeks and
try to kiss your loneliness.

I won't try more, because my life is sucked into
your hell and I am going to be in agony if I think
your smile depends on mine.

I can't make you happy,
I know your blood will be running out of passion
and the beats of your heart will be slow and
suddenly it will stop.

But my tiredness doesn't help, and your tears
hurt me as does the poison you want to try.

11.

You and I

create chaos

Chaos and stillness

create our poems

We together create oneness

12.

Today I surrendered to the pleasure of knowledge

but not that knowledge covered by words, anagrams and symbols

I surrender to the knowledge that is hidden in your hands and around your hair.

The wisdom I couldn't find in my books, not even in my poems,

it lies in your skin when it reacts to my soft touch,

it has been there all this time,

but my blindness keeps me away from truth.

It is in your kisses where I find my home,

finally, I have the knowledge of life, and the universe slips into your eyes each time when I love you.

13.

Start and finish with same sentence, she said.

Life is not like that

I welcome you

I thanked you

I loved you

When you left

I tried, I tried hard to say the same

But I just can say;

Please

Goodbye

And then try again

14.

You see me small, fragile and grey
you see me open and vulnerable
I ask you to run, don't look behind.

My shadows fly, my sorrow shouts loudly
You see me broken and down
You see me lost, damaged
I ask you to leave and never come back

But…

I woke this morning, hopeless and still weak
I woke up and then I received your kiss and a
fresh cup of coffee
You said; *I will stay because I know, you will rise
again.*

15.

My perfect lover is a blank piece of paper and
a full ink pen.
Nothing has been writing before there, but
everything can be read and understood.
There is no story, but experience is written on her
skin.
Her fingers don't have memories but curiosity,
they are ready to discover my world.

My perfect lover is living her life she does not
need mine.
She is free and does not need my wings,
She is in peace with her shadow and can walk
with my own.
Happy looking for the inanimate place where we
will meet again.

16.

Welcome to the unknown world,
the circus where the fools sleep and the puppets
dream.
Welcome to the magic vortex where everything
becomes true.
Where the chaos takes you and shakes your life
and fears.

Welcome to where the dust is not about your
aches but always about love.
Run away now, if you can't surrender to the idea
to let it go.
Run away or allow me to welcome you into the
unknown dimension where everything is
happening, and you can be lost.

17.

I wouldn't promise stillness

I don't know the meaning of it

I can promise you chaos where I used to live

It is located between the beating of my heart

and the bitterness of your lips.

18.

You came for a tea

Sat by my side

Stayed for a while

Just the time to steal my soul

You left a minute ago

Closed the door

Lost in your own thoughts

Just to justify why you killed my hope

19.

You celebrated my tears like the sky celebrates rain

The celebration of my sorrow was the taste of your success…

But the rain became a storm, the storm become a tornado

All of you was left behind

A rainbow was born, and I reclaimed my trophy

20.

Uncomfortable, unmentionable

is the passion between us

Uncomfortable for them

Unmentionable for us

It is the passion that grows inside our hearts.

21.

Feel the pain and cry

Because the end is just around

Around in your hands

Close to the end

Tomorrow is too late

Just say it

Before I say it

Don't pretend

We not have a second plan

22.

Silence is the winner

Between you and I

Words were never enough between us

Our bodies were the ones that said;

love you

Our bodies danced together along the floor to say; *goodbye.*

23.

Winter came early

Cold wind when it was supposed to be warm

How dare you dream a soft season when spring
is not even in the air?

Winter came early

Took your life and mine fell apart.

24.

Grief has so many faces;

The one that no one can see

because it is a loss that only you know,

that absence which only you will notice

because the person is around but far from your heart,

that person who became a ghost,

always walking around your home.

That love that is not coming back because it dies even if the person still breath and smile

25.

Can we make the dance start again?

Be mad in our own way

Dance like leaves in the wind

Lost in our own pace

26.

When my heart has fallen

Then

My soul raises its wings

27.

There is chaos, not only the one that you used to know.

There is a chaos but not the one that hurts your heart.

There is chaos but not the one that makes you anxious and desperate.

There is chaos the one that will be creating a new version of us.

There is a chaos, the magic one that created an exuberant dance.

There is chaos, a big bang of energy and love.

There is chaos, ready to explode in fulfilment and powerful desire.

Keep your eyes and heart wide open while,

this marvellous unexpected movement shows itself in newness.

28.

The station was quiet,

Few people walking slow

Delays, delays

The station was quiet,

Only one person walking slow

Late, it is late.

29.

It has only three letters

It will take only one second to pronounce it

It is lethal, cold

But it will liberate us.

END

30.

Today someone returned back to the soil

And someone came back to earth

Today there will be a sunrise

And then a sunset

Shorts cycles

Long cycles

Today I will be breathing in

Someone will be breathing out

Today a soul will be leaving us

A soul will be back

Ashes into space

Ashes back to the womb

31.

They give orders, instructions

Stop us, interrupt us

They send us away

Ask us to be quiet and

Not go too fast

They lock doors

Close the cage

They throw away the keys

They tell us what to say

How to dress and what to eat

It is not a prison

It is a school.

32.

We don't have power

      They do

We want to change things

      They don't

We don't have homes

      They do

We want to breathe

      They contaminate us.

33.

I tick one box

Then another box pops up

I ignored the new box

I erase the old box

Then another box pops up

I destroyed the new box

Then I become a box

34.

God, you are late

hell is a popular place

full of well-known faces, thinkers and creators.

You were just a few seconds over the time,

but late enough for all of us to go there.

35.

Is the hard weather what makes bird move?

Is it the hunter who makes animal feel insecure?

But there are angry hunters everywhere,

weapons are ready to kill, birds are ready to fly
high.

A second of distraction and you will be lost,

sleeping in the seductive hands of the unknown.

Weapons are ready, birds need to fly.

Avoiding the firing line is always a good move

If you don't want to be stock in a cage.

Is it the bad weather or the angry hunter who
makes birds move?

Are they birds, the ones that fly high to a place
that human eyes never reach?

Shoot your weapons, make the weather worse,
birds are safe, their spirit would never die.

36.

Labels lie
They say white when it is mixed,
there are more than two trees
there are more roots than the ones we can see.
Between positive and negative
I prefer the unknown neutral proton.
The box says *fragile*, when it is something
that has travelled far and fast to places that no-
one will ever know.
The signal says *stop* when we really need to run.

Labels lie
They say *right* when it is so wrong
The door says *entrance* when we are looking for
the exit
It says *welcome* when we have been invited to
leave
Never believe, labels lie
We live in a place with mirrors everywhere.
Mountains are there to be climbed
Rivers are there to be protected
We are here to be caregivers never to be
colonizers.

Labels lie
We are not humans
We are angels that fall
Super egos to be healed

37.

I am sorry

I forgot to say *adiós*

But yesterday, when the door no *abrió*

I realise that you also forgot about *nosotros* dos.

38.

Switch it on
Now
Switch it off
Take me out
Now
Pull me in
Lights are off
Now
Shout me down
Punch me hard
Kick me more
Now
Please
Switch it all off
Lights are too strong
I would try to
Breathe in and
Breathe out
But
I can just
Lie down

39.

What do I want to say?

You have asked many times

"I don't care", is my answer

This is what I want to say

Loud and clear

I don't care

I do what I do

Cause I don't care

I am who I am

Cause I want to

I don't care

Your barriers and your chains

Your jokes and your hate

No even your love or touch

I don't care, Not anymore

Free as I am to bring shame to myself

To fly and fall

To run and stop

Free as I am

40.

Things are not as we planned them

This is a hard time

Sometimes the hummingbird dies before the first
word becomes a poem.

41.

Whilst laughing, tears run through my face

Bliss is a mix between fullness and emptiness

To know that the mirror is enough

And realise that even it

Sometimes is too much.

There is no space, not any more

There is no time, not any more

To feel chains around my feet.

42.

Sit at my dinner table

Thinking about changing the world

my stomach feels empty

But my mind is full

What a good feeling my god!

The coffee is still hot

And I haven't moved. It will rain tomorrow, they said

I just remembered I don't have umbrella, not even a hat

But my heart is not broken

What a good feeling my god!

43.

We all have the seeds of evilness

we just see what is unimportant

blindness and deafness

we just listen to the dust in the air after the storm.

44.

Once and twice

I can start again and again

I can see the sun

Face my ghosts

Light up the fire

Protect myself from the wild beast

Scare my own shadow

Once and twice

Because I know what is running

In my blood

What is waiting in my bowels

The information I carry

In my bones

The inspiration in my soul

Once and twice

You can try but

I will stand up again

Printed in Great Britain
by Amazon

22454507R00057